# OLD TESTAMENT

## *God's Unfolding Promise*

Phil Campbell and
Bryson Smith

**FAITHWALK**
BIBLE STUDIES

CROSSWAY BOOKS • WHEATON, ILLINOIS
A DIVISION OF GOOD NEWS PUBLISHERS

*Old Testament: God's Unfolding Promise*

Copyright © 1997, 2000 by St. Matthias Press, Ltd.

First U. S. edition published 2000 by Crossway Books
a division of Good News Publishers
1300 Crescent Street
Wheaton, Illinois 60187

First published 1997 in Australia by Matthias Media under the title
*Full of Promise.*

Cover design: David LaPlaca

Cover photo: The Stock Market

Printed in the United States of America

ISBN 1-58134-145-8

| 15 | 14 | 13 | 12 | 11 | 10 | 09 | 08 | 07 | 06 | 05 | 04 | 03 | 02 | 01 | 00 |
|----|----|----|----|----|----|----|----|----|----|----|----|----|----|----|----|
| 15 | 14 | 13 | 12 | 11 | 10 | 9 | 8 | 7 | 6 | 5 | 4 | 3 | 2 | 1 | |

# Contents

# How to Make the Most of These Studies

## 1. What Is an Interactive Bible Study?

These "interactive" Bible studies are a bit like a guided tour of a famous city. The studies will take you through the Old Testament, pointing out things along the way, filling in background details, and suggesting avenues for further exploration. But there is also time for you to do some sightseeing of your own—to wander off, have a good look for yourself, and form your own conclusions.

In other words, we have designed these studies to fall halfway between a sermon and a set of unadorned Bible study questions. We want to provide stimulation and input and point you in the right direction, while leaving you to do a lot of the exploration and discovery yourself.

We hope that these studies will stimulate a lot of interaction—interaction with the Bible, with the teaching material, with your own ideas, with other people in discussion, and with God as you talk to Him about it all.

## 2. The Format

Each study contains sections of text to introduce, summarize, suggest, and provoke. Interspersed throughout the teaching are three types of "interaction," each with its own symbol:

**STARTING OUT**

Questions to help you think about society and your own experience in a way that tunes you in to the issues being raised by the Bible passage.

**FINDING TRUTH**

Questions to help you investigate key parts of the Bible.

**GOING FURTHER**

Questions to help you think through the implications of your discoveries.

When you come to one of these symbols, you'll know that it's time to do some work on your own.

## 3. Suggestions for Individual Study

▲ Before you begin, pray that God will open your eyes to what He is saying in His Word and give you the strength to do something about it. You may be spurred to pray again at the end of the study.

▲ Work through the study, following the directions as you go. Write in the spaces provided.

▲ Resist the temptation to skip over the *Starting Out, Finding Truth,* and *Going Further* sections. It is important to think about the sections of text (rather than just accepting them as true) and to ponder the implications for your life. Writing these things down is a valuable way to get your thoughts working.

▲ Take what opportunities you can to talk with others about what you've learned.

## 4. Suggestions for Group Study

▲ Much of what we have suggested above applies to group study as well. The studies are suitable for structured Bible study or cell groups, as well as for more informal pairs and threesomes.

Get together with one or more friends and work on the studies at your own pace. You don't need the formal structure of a "group" to gain maximum benefit.

▲ It is vital that group members work through the study themselves *before* the group meets. The group discussion can take place comfortably in an hour (depending on how sidetracked you get!), but only if all the members have done the work and are familiar with the material.

▲ Spend most of the group time discussing the "interactive" sections—*Starting Out, Finding Truth,* and *Going Further.* Reading all the text together would take too long and should be unnecessary if group members have done their preparation. You may wish to underline and read aloud particular paragraphs or sections of text that you think are important.

▲ The role of the group leader is to direct the course of the discussion and try to draw the threads together at the end. This will mean a little extra preparation—underlining important sections of text to emphasize, deciding which questions are worth concentrating on, being sure of the main thrust of the study. Leaders will also probably want to decide approximately how long they'd like to spend on each part.

▲ We haven't included an "answer guide" to the questions in the studies. This is a deliberate move—we want to give you a guided tour of the Old Testament, not a lecture. There is more than enough in the text we have written and the questions we have asked to point you in what we think is the right direction. The rest is up to you.

▲ For more input, see "Tips for Leaders" at the end of the book.

# 1

# When Good Turns Bad

## GENESIS 1–11

 **STARTING OUT**

Without looking at a Bible, draw a diagram or a time line containing what you see as the main events of the Old Testament. (Use space on facing page.)

### The Big Picture

Jigsaw puzzles are great fun. At least that's what people keep saying. Some of us, however, find them hard work. Sitting at a table surrounded by hundreds of little pieces of colored cardboard only confuses and frustrates us.

The way many of us feel about jigsaw puzzles may also be the way we feel about the Old Testament. We may know lots of individual pieces of the Old Testament, like Daniel in the lions' den or David and Goliath, but we're not really sure how all these stories fit together. In fact some of us may not even know that they do fit together at all! The end result is that the Old Testament can be a confusing and frustrating part of the Bible which we either avoid altogether or dip into at random like a phone book or a dictionary.

The aim of this study book is to take some of the confusion out of the Old Testament by providing an overview of its main themes and events. The studies will be like taking a scenic flight over a spectacular but varied landscape. From the plane we'll be able to see the main points of interest—but of course we won't have the time to land and study many things in detail.

By the time our flight is over, however, we will hopefully have gained an appreciation of the overall landscape and how it all fits together. That's a particularly important thing to do with the Old Testament, because the events of this part of the Bible prepare us for the greatest event in the history of this planet: the life, death, and resurrection of Jesus Christ.

The big question is, where do we start? There are so many different people, places, and events. Which should we look at first? Well, believe it or not, when it comes to the Old Testament, the best place to start is at the beginning.

 **FINDING TRUTH**

1.  Quickly read through Genesis 1:1–2:3. Do you notice any recurring words or phrases?

2.  What do you think these patterns tell us about God and the world?

3.  What words or phrases in these verses reflect the fact that humanity has a special place in God's plans?

## A Good Creation

We have discovered that the Old Testament opens with God creating a good world. God is seen as a powerful and systematic Creator. First God separates all the different compartments of creation, and then He methodically fills each compartment with appropriate things. For example, the land and water are first separated, and then the water is filled with sea creatures and the land is filled with vegetation and animals.

Genesis reveals a Creator who has a place for everything, and who puts everything in its place. This world has a design and purpose. We are not here by accident!

Within God's design for creation, humanity has a central role. Man is created to be God's representative on earth, placed here to enjoy fellowship with God and to care for the creation. In this respect, God's creative work culminates in His "rest" on the seventh day. The seventh day is a picture of God and humanity enjoying perfect rest together in an unspoiled world.

 **FINDING TRUTH**

1.  Genesis 3 records the rebellion of Adam and Eve against God's rule. This is often called "the Fall." Read Genesis 3:1-7. How is the Fall typical of all sin?

2.  Read Genesis 3:8-24. In these verses, God punishes Adam and Eve for their rebellion. But things have changed. How is the created order now different?

## A Bad Decision

As the story of Genesis unfolds, God's good creation is tainted by sin. In Genesis 3, Adam and Eve take life into their own hands, and instead of following God's good instructions they make up their own rules and decide to eat from the tree of the knowledge of good and evil. This rebellious act immediately introduces tension, mistrust, and antagonism into all levels of what had been a good creation.

Mankind is now engaged in a struggle with nature. Man and woman are now engaged in a struggle with each other. Even at one of humanity's most beautiful and treasured moments, the birth of a child, there is now pain and anguish! All because humanity thought it knew better than God.

And the bad news is only just beginning!

**FINDING TRUTH**

1. Skim through Genesis 4–11, noting the main events. How do they show the spread of sin and the worsening of creation?

2. Despite all the bad things that happen in Genesis 4–11, is there any evidence that God is still actively blessing His creation?

## The Spread of Sin

We're only eleven chapters into the Old Testament, but already things seem to be going from bad to worse. Things started out so well, with God, mankind, and nature in harmony within a good creation, but before long the whole world unravels into murder, incest, violence, deceit, and corruption. Indeed, by the time we reach the end of chapter 11, we begin to wonder why God even puts up with us.

Despite this escalation of sin and evil in the world, there are still signs that God is at work blessing His creation and trying to rectify things. For example, even in the midst of judging sin by means of the Flood, God graciously rescues one man and his family. God even blesses Noah with words very similar to those He spoke to Adam and Eve (Gen. 9:1-3). We are seeing God's tenacious commitment to His creation. Even when mankind is repeatedly unfaithful, God keeps faithfully working to reverse the effects of the Fall.

This is an exciting discovery about God for, as we will see, it leads us straight to Jesus Christ!

## GOING FURTHER

1. Genesis describes God as a powerful and loving Creator. Look up the following passages and consider how this truth should shape our lives:

   ▲ Psalm 104

   ▲ Luke 12:22-34

2. "I believe that God is nature. God is the living earth—that's why we should look after our environment." How would you respond to that comment?

3. According to Romans 1:20, what can we tell about God from creation? What areas of creation help you personally to appreciate the greatness of God?

4.  Because of the Fall, life in the world is a mixture of good and bad, achievement and frustration. In what specific areas of life are you feeling this?

5.  What was Jesus Christ's role in creation? What do the following passages say about how this should affect the way we respond to Christ?

    ▲ John 1:1-3

    ▲ Colossians 1:15-17

    ▲ Hebrews 1:3

6.  On a scale of 1 to 10 (with 10 being the highest) how would you rate God's faithfulness to His creation?

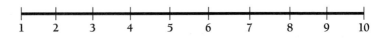

7.  From what you've seen so far, how would you rate mankind's faithfulness to God? Mark your rating on the scale below.

# 2

# *Promises, Promises*

## GENESIS 12–50

 **STARTING OUT**

You're stopped in the street by a TV reporter who asks for your opinion on what's wrong with this world. How would you answer?

## A New Start

"Do we renovate or demolish?" It's a question hundreds of homeowners ask themselves each year. Do we improve the kitchen, update the bathroom, and add a couple of extra rooms? Or is it easier to just pull the whole house down and build a completely new one? Do we renovate or demolish?

In Genesis 9 to 11, that's the question God has been asking about His creation. We've discovered that things started out well. In Genesis

1, God made a good creation in which He, humanity, and nature all related harmoniously. But humanity rebelled against God's rule, and as a result creation spiraled into a cycle of sin and punishment. Indeed, even though God has almost demolished the world already and made a new start with Noah, by the time we reach the Tower of Babel (Gen. 11) humanity has again degenerated into an arrogant, self-assertive community that tries to force its way into heaven itself! The rot runs very, very deep.

So what is God to do? Is there a workable way to renovate creation, or should He demolish His world once and for all? Can humanity be repaired? Or is it simply better to destroy absolutely everything and start again? Let's see what God decides.

 **FINDING TRUTH**

1. Read Genesis 12:1-9.

   a. What does God promise Abram in these verses?

   b. Compare Genesis 11:4 with 12:2. What do these verses tell us about humanity and God?

2.  In Genesis 15, God repeats His promises to Abram. Read verses 1-6. What new things do we discover about God and Abram in these verses?

3.  How do God's promises to Abram reflect a return to the good creation of Genesis 1–2?

## Eden Revisited

Remarkably, surprisingly, graciously, God chooses to repair the sin in creation by means of certain promises to Abram. Specifically (in Gen. 12:1-3), God promises:

1.  that Abram's descendants will increase and become a great nation (to reflect this promise, God changes Abram's name to Abraham, which means "father of many");
2.  to give Abraham's descendants their own special land;
3.  to bless Abraham's descendants, and that they in turn will bring blessing to all people.

God's promises to Abraham are majestic acts of grace, because through them God is committing Himself to reversing the effects of the Fall. Just as God created Adam and Eve, placed them in a special land, and blessed them, He now promises to create a new people whom He will also put in a special land and bless. Through His promises to Abraham, God is vowing to bring into existence a new humanity in which the curses of the Fall will be replaced with blessing.

**FINDING TRUTH**

1. The remainder of Genesis details the next few generations of Abraham's family, coming to a climax with the story of Joseph. Skim through your Bible and note some of the main events in these chapters. As you do, draw a family tree from Abraham to Joseph.

| Main Events | Family Tree |
|---|---|
| | |

2. How do the events in these chapters relate to God's promises to Abraham?

3. Read Joseph's last words in Genesis 50:24-25. How does Genesis end in relation to God's promises?

## Abraham and the Rest of the Old Testament

God's promises to Abraham are of great importance in the Bible. They are promises to undo the effects of the Fall. They are promises to renovate the world and take life back to a Garden of Eden experience. These promises form the backbone of the rest of the Old Testament. Everything that happens in the Old Testament from Genesis 12 onward has God's promises to Abraham in view. That is essentially what we're going to discover in the remainder of this book. In every study we will see God working to fulfill His promises to Abraham. The great tragedy, however, is that in every study we will also see how mankind's unfaithfulness keeps working against God's desire to reverse the Fall.

## Abraham, Jesus, and Us

The most exciting thing about the Old Testament is that it prepares us for Jesus Christ. Time and time again throughout these studies we will discover ways in which the Old Testament points forward to the coming of Christ. This is especially the case with God's promises to Abraham.

The New Testament depicts Jesus Christ as the ultimate fulfillment of all of God's promises (2 Cor. 1:20). God's promises to Abraham are no exception. Christ brings into existence a people of God who have a special inheritance that will not fade, and who have been blessed with every spiritual blessing. In so doing, it is Jesus Christ who reverses the Fall and fulfills God's promises to Abraham.

 **GOING FURTHER**

1. In the New Testament, Abraham is also considered an important person. Look up the following passages and consider how Abraham helps us better understand how we are saved by Christ.

   ▲ Romans 4

   ▲ Galatians 4:21-31 (for the adventurous)

   ▲ Hebrews 11:8-12

2.  We, like Abraham, are saved by trust in God's promises. This is quite a surprising way to be saved. What are some other ways that people think they can be put right with God?

3.  When is it hard to trust God?

4.  What things can we do to strengthen our trust in God? Be specific.

5.  "God doesn't care about the world. If He did He would have done something about all the evil things that happen!" How would you respond to that comment?

6. We've now reached the end of Genesis. Again, give God's faithfulness a rating from 1 to 10.

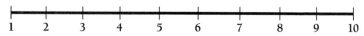

7. Abraham and his descendants are now the focal point of God's dealings with mankind. From what you've seen in this study, give them a score for their faithfulness to God.

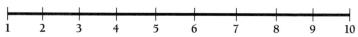

# 3

# The Great Escape

## EXODUS–DEUTERONOMY

 **STARTING OUT**

Write a brief summary of the book of Genesis.

## Escapes and Rescue Missions

As he lay recovering in the hospital, Ross McGill was surrounded by TV cameras. The eyes of all Australia were on him. He was a survivor. More than that, he was a hero. After his helicopter crashed in a dry creekbed, Ross dragged himself on his hands and knees through the Australian desert for more than twelve hours to raise the alarm and save his friends. It was a dramatic rescue. It was a great escape, against incredible odds. Don't you just love stories like that?

If you enjoy escape stories, you're going to love this study, because we've reached the greatest escape of the Old Testament.

The escape is called the "Exodus," and through it God, in a display of awesome power, rescues more than 600,000 people from slavery and oppression. But it's not just the scale of the escape that makes the Exodus so significant. The Exodus is critically important to what happens in the rest of the Old Testament. Indeed, if we don't understand the Exodus, there is much in the rest of the Bible that we won't fully appreciate, including the death and resurrection of Jesus Christ.

**FINDING TRUTH**

By the end of Genesis, Joseph (Abraham's great-grandson) had become a man of great power in Egypt. Through Joseph's influence all of Abraham's descendants had settled in Egypt so as to survive a severe famine. Exodus details the events following Joseph's time.

1. Read Exodus 1:6-11. What link can you see with God's promises to Abraham? (What parts of the promise do you see being fulfilled?)

2. Abraham's descendants, the Israelites, are persecuted by Pharaoh and subjected to slavery. Read Exodus 2:23-24; 3:15-17. What does God plan to do and why?

3. Pharaoh refuses to let Israel go, despite numerous plagues sent from God. Eventually God sends one last terrible plague. Quickly skim Exodus 12:1-41. What eventually forced Pharaoh to let Israel go?

## The Birth of a Nation

The book of Exodus opens with things not looking too good for Abraham's descendants. The Israelites have indeed become very numerous, but there still seems to be a long way to go before God's promises to Abraham are fulfilled. In particular, the people of Israel aren't really galvanized into a nation yet. That's why the Exodus is such an important event.

In the Exodus, God begins to fulfill His promise to Abraham by forming Israel into a unified, distinct nation which is on its way to the Promised Land. The Exodus marks the start of the Jewish nation, and throughout the nation's history the Exodus was to be Israel's reference point for everything. To be a Jew meant to identify yourself with this great escape. That's why the Exodus was to mark the start of the Jewish calendar (Ex. 12:2).

As well as the Exodus being the beginning of the Israelite nation, the Bible also emphasizes certain characteristics of the way the Israelites were rescued:

### ▲ A lamb is sacrificed

When God saw the blood of the sacrificed lamb on the Israelite doors, He passed over the house. The death of that innocent lamb took the place of the death of their own firstborn.

### ▲ God did it

National Israel did not come into existence through its own efforts. It's not that Israel waged war against Egypt and eventually won its freedom. Israel was released from slavery because God did it!

### ▲ From slavery to freedom

Israel had been oppressed and enslaved in Egypt, and now it was free. God heard its cry and remembered His promises. He freed the nation. Its slavery was ended.

### ▲ From poverty to riches

The Exodus also meant going from poverty to riches. It wasn't as if the Israelites only managed to get out with the clothes on their backs. They walked away with the treasure of Egypt in their suitcases; the Egyptians *gave* it to them!

On any terms, this is an incredible escape. Through the sacrificial death of a lamb God took His people from slavery and poverty to freedom and great riches. It is the greatest escape of the Old Testament. But it is not the greatest escape of the Bible! There's one other escape in the Bible that's even more phenomenal. But more of that later. Let's first see what happens to Israel now that they have been set free.

**FINDING TRUTH**

1.  After freeing the people of Israel from their oppression, God gathers them together at Mount Sinai and explains His further plans. Read Exodus 19:3-8.

    a.  What is God going to do with Israel, and how do these plans relate to His promises to Abraham?

    b.  What do the Israelites say they'll do?

2.  Read Exodus 16:1-3; 17:1-2; and 32:1-4. Despite what they said, has the Israelites' behavior improved?

3.  Skim quickly through the contents of Exodus 24–40. What do these chapters seem to be mainly about? Why do you think this receives so much attention?

4.  How does Exodus end (Ex. 40:34-38)? How does this ending relate to God's promises to Abraham?

## Leviticus and Numbers

After the Exodus, God gathers His people around Mount Sinai and gives them numerous laws relating to their life as the people of God.

The latter chapters of Exodus give a great deal of attention to the planning and construction of a moveable tabernacle (or tent) in which God will dwell as His people move toward the Promised Land. The tabernacle is a sign of God's deep desire to involve Himself with His people and bless them. To have the Creator of the universe living among them is an extraordinary privilege.

The record of the giving of God's laws carries on through Leviticus, as Moses teaches the people of Israel how to stand in proper awe of God's mercy and holiness. If Israel is to be a nation with God living within it as King, certain matters of "royal protocol" must be observed.

In the book of Numbers, the Israelites finally leave Mount Sinai and move to the edge of the Promised Land. They send spies into the Promised Land to help plan the invasion. But things don't go well. The spies bring back stories of fierce inhabitants in the land, and the Israelites become afraid. Out of fear they refuse to enter the land God has promised them. This is essentially an act of mistrust in God, and so, as discipline, God decrees that Israel will wander the desert for forty years. During this time of wandering, God miraculously provides for Israel with food, drink, and sandals that don't wear out! God is teaching His people that He is faithful and is worthy of their trust.

At the end of this time of wandering, Israel again gathers at the edge of the Promised Land for a second attempt at entering. The book of Deuteronomy is made up of three speeches Moses gives just before this second attempt.

 **FINDING TRUTH**

1. Read Deuteronomy 7:7-9. Why is God doing what He is doing?

2. Read Deuteronomy 6:4-15. What should Israel's response be?

3. Read Deuteronomy 7:1-4. What specific things should Israel do to safeguard their wholehearted allegiance to God?

4. As they prepare to enter the Promised Land, the Israelites need to be reminded that their permanent possession of the land isn't automatic. In fact, in Deuteronomy 29 Moses paints a vivid picture of the possible horrors of exile from the land. He imagines a future where horrified onlookers will ask, "Why has the Lord done this?" If the terrible things Moses describes were to actually happen, what would be the answer to this question? (See Deut. 29:25-28.)

5. Moses gives the Israelites a clear choice. Look at Deuteronomy 30:15-20. What are Israel's options?

**On the Edge**

We leave this study with Israel now poised on the edge of the Promised Land, ready for their second attempt at entering. As we have noted several times already, Israel is here, at the border of Canaan, only by virtue of God's gracious promises to Abraham. God is faithfully keeping His promises to form Abraham's descendants into a great nation, to bless them, and to settle them in their own special land. Yet despite God's generosity, the Israelites have been grumbling and complaining every step of the way.

In our next study we'll consider whether or not things improve once the Israelites actually get into the Promised Land—and we'll be watching to see to what extent they heed Moses' warnings. Before we leave this study however, there are exciting things for us to see about Jesus.

## The Greatest Escape

Before the present Australian Parliament House was built in Canberra, it was possible to visit a model of the proposed building. The model was a beautifully presented miniature, housed in its own special display center. But as impressive as the model was, its purpose was to point to the final structure. The model had a role to play, but it obviously paled into insignificance alongside the real thing.

That is how Jesus treats the Exodus. The night before His death, as He was celebrating the Passover festival with His disciples, Jesus explained that He had come to fulfill the Passover. In fact, His disciples were to replace the Passover meal with a meal in remembrance of Him (Luke 22). In other words, the Exodus may be the greatest escape in the Old Testament—but it is not the greatest escape in the Bible. The Exodus was a prelude, a foreshadowing of the rescue that Christ would achieve on the Cross. As such, all four characteristics that we noted earlier about the Exodus find their fulfillment in a much more radical sense through the death of Jesus, the Lamb of God, who died to free us from our slavery.

 **GOING FURTHER**

1. Consider how each of these characteristics of the Exodus finds its fulfillment in Christ:

    ▲ A lamb is sacrificed (see John 1:29; Rev. 5:6-10)


    ▲ God did it (see Eph. 2:4-9)


    ▲ From slavery to freedom (see Rom. 8:1-4; Gal. 5:1-6)


    ▲ From poverty to riches (see 2 Cor. 8:9; Eph. 1:3, 18)

2.  In Hebrews 3:7-13, Israel is presented as an example for us *not* to follow. In what specific ways can we encourage each other not to harden our hearts against God?

3.  Moses urged Israel never to forget the Exodus, since it was the event that gave them their identity. The same is true of the Cross for us. What steps can we take never to forget the Cross? What things can threaten to push our attention away from Christ?

4.  We've covered quite a lot of material in this study. Is there any one section that you have found particularly interesting or helpful or instructive? Why?

5.  God's faithfulness rating is still stuck firmly on 10, but the Israelites can be a frustrating bunch! Give them an updated rating for their faithfulness to God.

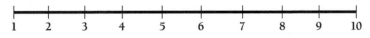

1    2    3    4    5    6    7    8    9    10

# 4

# Great Expectations

## JOSHUA–1 SAMUEL

 **STARTING OUT**

Imagine that you're an Israelite living during the time of Deuteronomy. You've been wandering in the desert for forty years, during which time you have seen an entire generation die out. Moses is dead, and Joshua is your new leader. You are about to cross the Jordan into the land that God promised to Abraham's descendants. How do you feel and why?

## Looking Forward to a Land

Melissa's hands trembled with excitement as she sat in the theater seat. What a night! Other performances had come and gone, but she'd never been able to get a seat. Either the tickets had been too expensive or else they had sold out before she could get one. But this time was different. Melissa had been saving for the ticket for months. She had stood in line for hours waiting for the box office to open so that she could get the best seat in the house. Tonight was the big night. The curtain lifted. Melissa's pulse quickened.

Most of us know the feelings of excited anticipation that occur when an event we've been looking forward to finally happens. That's how we should be feeling as the curtain opens on the book of Joshua. Israel is finally about to set foot into the Promised Land!

It hasn't always looked as if Israel would get to this point. A powerful Pharaoh had opposed their release from slavery. Acts of disobedience had resulted in Israel wandering in the desert for forty years of discipline. Yet through it all God has been astonishingly faithful to His promises to Abraham. God has made Israel into a numerous people. Now they are poised to take possession of the land that God promised Abraham. Expectations are great. Let's see how they do.

 **FINDING TRUTH**

1. The book of Joshua details the initial conquests of the Promised Land. Look at Joshua 1:1-7.

   a. Why is God giving them the land?


   b. What does He expect from the Israelites and Joshua in return?


2. Look up the following verses in Joshua. How are the people responding to God?

   ▲ 7:1


   ▲ 9:14-15


   ▲ 17:12-13


   ▲ 18:1-3


   ▲ 24:19-24

3. Read Joshua 24:28-33. How does the book of Joshua conclude? What has been achieved so far concerning God's promises?

## Joshua

In high school, we learned about continental drift, the process by which land masses are slowly moving across the surface of the earth. It's far too slow to notice, but it's so powerful that it can cause an entire mountain range to form.

In Joshua we encounter "relationship drift," as Israel drifts away from God. It's almost too slow to notice at first, but it's happening—and it can have catastrophic results. The book of Joshua has so many positive events in it, as city after city is conquered by the Israelites, that it's possible to miss the signs of relationship drift. But as the book unfolds, the Israelites become more and more apathetic about God. This is shown by their failure to totally remove the Canaanites from the land they're moving into, even though God has repeatedly commanded them to do so, promising to give them victory if they follow Him.

All this is very disappointing. Joshua started out with great expectations. The Israelites were entering the Promised Land, and God had promised to care for them there. It was as if the Garden of Eden experience was going to happen all over again—God's people in God's place being blessed by God. Sadly, it wasn't working out all that well.

Perhaps things will get better.

 **FINDING TRUTH**

1. The book of Judges describes the "mopping-up operations" in the land of Canaan. There are still plenty of idolatrous and pagan tribes to be driven out. Throughout this time, Israel is unique among the nations because it doesn't have a political king. Instead it is led by "judges."

    Read Judges 2:10-19 and draw a diagram to represent what's happening during this period of history.

2. Read Judges 8:22-23. What is the significance of the fact that the Israelites don't have a human king?

3. Read Judges 3:1-4. What is God doing with His people during this time?

4. What is the result? (Judg. 3:7; 3:12; 4:1; 6:1; 13:1)

5. What state is Israel in by the end of the book? (see 21:25)

## Judges and 1 Samuel

Israel's disobedience is starting to gather speed. The Israelites are continually flirting with other gods and compromising their relationship with the one true God. Even the judges themselves reflect a steady decline in quality. By the time we meet Samson at the end of the book of Judges, he seems nothing more than an arrogant womanizer who is interested in saving Israel only when it benefits his love life!

In many ways, Samson provides a picture of Israel in miniature. Just as Samson compromises his allegiance to God by repeatedly seeking after foreign women, Israel compromises her allegiance to

God by repeatedly seeking after foreign gods. The signs are not good for Israel. Samson eventually dies as a prisoner at the hands of his enemies. Will the same happen to Israel?

The story continues in the books of 1 and 2 Samuel.

 **FINDING TRUTH**

1. Samuel was the last of the judges. Although he was a godly man, his sons were not. Israel falls into a state of decay. In an attempt to restore their fortunes, the people make an important request in 1 Samuel 8. What do they ask for and why?

2. What is God's response?

3. What does God specifically warn them of?

4. Saul is chosen as the first king of Israel, a choice God promotes in order to teach the Israelites something of the perils of human kingship. However, God's real aim is to bless His people, and so in 1 Samuel 16:1-13, God selects the ideal king. Who is it, and why is his elevation to the kingship unexpected?

5. Read 1 Samuel 31:1-7. What is the condition of Israel by the end of the book?

## What's Wrong with Israel?

In this study we have covered the main events of Israel's settlement in the Promised Land, as described in the books of Joshua, Judges, and 1 Samuel. All in all, it's a pretty sorry tale. Israel entered the Promised Land with high hopes, but through repeated sin and rebellion they are now a shattered people at the mercy of the Philistines.

Throughout this segment of their history, the problem with Israel is that they want all the blessings from God but are unprepared for the responsibilities that go with those blessings. They refuse to follow God wholeheartedly. They want God's blessings on their own terms, rather than on God's terms. They settle in the land among the Canaanites rather than removing them as God wanted. They presume on God's grace, taking an interest in God only when things get difficult and they need help. They even decide to have a king so that they can be like the other nations. All this is a rejection of God as their ruler.

In many ways this sad period of history is like the Fall all over again. God's people are in God's land, but they are rejecting God's way of life. Adam and Eve were expelled from the garden because of their rebellion. What will the future hold for Israel in the Promised Land of Canaan?

## God's Faithfulness

If there is a ray of hope in this gloomy period of Israelite history, it is the way in which God's surprising grace continually shines through. Despite His frustration with human sin, God remains at work. Certainly He uses some rather unexpected people and unexpected weapons, but through it all God consistently works to save Israel from her enemies so as to fulfill His promises. Even when a judge actually dies, as in the case of Samson, God is still powerfully at work saving His people (e.g., Judg. 16:30).

This is a part of the Old Testament, therefore, that makes us look forward to a new Joshua, a new Judge, a new King, to a person who will not fail but will conquer God's enemies once for all. That person, of course, is Jesus Christ. In Him we will finally meet the solution to all humanity's problems, and the answer to all God's promises.

 **GOING FURTHER**

1. Israel's rejection of God is revealed by its chasing after the gods of the Canaanites. What false gods do we frequently chase after? What specific things can we do to protect ourselves?

2. After all that God had done for them, why do you think Israel so quickly deserted Him in the Promised Land? What lessons can we learn?

3. Read Joshua 1:9. In what way, if any, do these words to Joshua have relevance for us?

4. During the time of the judges, God has used some unexpected people and weapons to defeat His enemies. How is this also true of Christ?

5. As we have seen in this study, Israel's faithfulness to God has been a bit wobbly. How do you think their faithfulness rating is going?

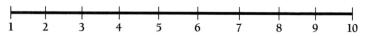

1   2   3   4   5   6   7   8   9   10

# 5

# *The Kingdom Comes*

## David–Solomon

 **STARTING OUT**

1.  Congratulations! We are now halfway through our studies on the Old Testament. If a friend who hadn't been doing these studies asked you, "What's the Old Testament all about?" what would you say?

2.  Think back to before you started these studies. In what ways is your answer different now than it would have been back then?

## But Wait—There's More!

You've seen the ads on TV. Maybe you've even bought the products. "But wait—there's more! Order this amazing new combination CD storage rack and orange juicer today, and you'll receive these incredible steak knives at no extra cost. And that's not all . . ."

Trouble is, when the package arrives in the mail, it's mostly junk. The steak knives are blunt, the orange juice squirts all over your CD collection, and you finally realize that what you got wasn't nearly as good as what you were promised.

But where God is concerned, His promises never disappoint. So far in our studies we've been following the fulfillment of God's promises to Abraham. But as we'll discover in this study, God is not content merely to keep His promises to Abraham. There's more. And it really does get better and better! As it becomes evident that God's promises to Abraham are finally being fulfilled in the land of Israel, God makes new promises to add blessing on top of blessing.

 **FINDING TRUTH**

After a time of internal political turmoil in Israel, things have finally settled down. David is king, Jerusalem is his capital city, and he's living in style in a cedar-lined palace. But that's just the start of the good things God has in mind.

1.   Read 2 Samuel 7:1-17.

    a.   What does David want to build?

    b.   What does God want to do first?

    c.   Who has been responsible for David's "good fortune" so far? (vv. 8-9)

d. What does the future hold for David and his family? (vv. 9, 11-15)

e. What does the future hold for Israel? (v. 10)

f. What similarities can you see between the promises God is making to David and His earlier promises to Abraham?

g. What new features have been added?

h. As usual, we'll need to keep in mind the incredible ability we humans have to mess things up. What small hint of possible future problems do you notice among these promises? (Keep this in mind!)

2. Read David's response to God's promises, in 2 Samuel 7:18-29. David knows that God's new promises to him (vv. 1-17) are not of the cheap, "free-steak-knives" type! David is dumbfounded by the sheer magnitude and scope of God's generosity toward him.

If someone had asked David to summarize the story of the Old Testament so far, which verses in this section do you think would make up his answer?

## David's Son

God has some great plans for David and his family. For starters, He's made the remarkable promise that David's descendants will rule God's people forever! As a first step, David's son will build the temple David has wanted to build. The symbol of God's dwelling place with His people will become a permanent focus for the people of Israel. And, most remarkable of all, there will be a special bond between God and Israel's king. "I will be his father," says God, "and he will be my son" (2 Sam. 7:14).

Ominously, though, God already anticipates more sin and failure. And when it happens, there will be consequences: "When he does wrong, I will punish him with the rod of men, with floggings inflicted by men" (2 Sam. 7:14b). Even so, God promises to remain faithful. His love will remain with David's line forever, no matter what.

The next few chapters (2 Sam. 8–10) describe how the kingdom of Israel is consolidated under David's rule. Surrounding tribes fall like dominoes and become subject to his rule. Tributes and gifts of precious gold and useful bronze flow in from every direction.

But there's a fatal flaw. David commits a big-time sin, and the consequences will haunt his family for generations. David's spur-of-the-moment adulterous affair with the beautiful Bathsheba leads him also to have her innocent husband murdered. The rest of 2 Samuel reads like a sleazy soap opera, with the royal family of Israel racked by family feuds, rivalry, and murderous ambition. It's brother against brother in an eerie reminder of the relationship between Cain and Abel outside of Eden. Surely life in the Promised Land should be better than this!

For a moment, at least, it is. Surprisingly, Bathsheba, the wife gained through David's deception, gives birth to the son who will bear God's blessing. His name is Solomon, and under his rule Israel enters a golden era of peace and prosperity.

 **FINDING TRUTH**

1. Read 1 Kings 3:1-15. Sounds promising, doesn't it? Solomon is king, and when God speaks to him in a dream and offers to fulfill his greatest wish, Solomon asks for something far better than a big palace, a fast chariot, or a winning ticket in the Egyptian lottery.

a. What hints can you see from verses 6 to 8 that Solomon has God's long-standing promises in mind?

b. What is Solomon's request?

c. What is God's response?
▲ v. 12

▲ v. 13

2. Look up the following references and consider which promise of God is being fulfilled.
▲ 1 Kings 4:20

▲ 1 Kings 4:21

▲ 1 Kings 6:1-3

▲ 1 Kings 10:4-9

## A Palace for Solomon, a House for God

If David's kingdom was glorious, Solomon's was even more glorious. Under Solomon's rule the Promised Land is firmly settled, Israel is elevated to the status of a world power, and even Gentile rulers such as the Queen of Sheba praise the God of Israel. It seems that the promises to Abraham have finally come true.

But there's more! God's promises to David also seem to be coming to fulfillment. Solomon becomes the first king of Israel who achieves his rule through birthright. Furthermore, he succeeds in building the temple in Jerusalem to replace the tabernacle as God's symbolic dwelling place in the midst of His people.

But there's even more! Solomon has asked God for wisdom, and God says yes! In fact, God gives Solomon the works—he gets the things he didn't ask for as well, such as prosperity and honor.

These are great days, and this mood of excitement is reflected by Solomon's moving prayer at the dedication of the temple (1 Kings 8), a prayer that points us back to the great covenant promises of God. Take a look, for example, at these words in verses 23 and 24:

*"O LORD, God of Israel, there is no God like you in heaven above or on earth below—you who keep your covenant of love with your servants who continue wholeheartedly in your way. You have kept your promise to your servant David my father; with your mouth you have promised and with your hand you have fulfilled it—as it is today."*

Or how about verse 56:

*"Praise be to the LORD, who has given rest to his people Israel just as he promised. Not one word has failed of all the good promises he gave through his servant Moses."*

This truly is the golden age of Israel. The big question is, will Solomon practice what he preaches? Is Solomon someone whose heart is "fully committed to the Lord our God"? Scratch the surface, and what sort of king do you find? In the next study, we'll find out. But for now, notice some small, disturbing signs.

 **FINDING TRUTH**

1.  Read 1 Kings 6:38–7:1. As well as building the temple, Solomon builds himself an impressive new palace. Which building project took longest?

2.  Compare the dimensions of the temple (1 Kings 6:2) with the dimensions of the palace (7:2). Which is the more impressive building? What might this reveal about Solomon's priorities?

3.  Look back at 1 Kings 3:14. What is the condition attached to God's promise of wisdom?

4.  Look further back, to 1 Kings 3:1-4. Are there any hints here that Solomon might have been heading for trouble? List them.

5.  Look even further back, to Deuteronomy 17:16-17. Long before Solomon was even a speck on the horizon of history, God had given some very clear guidelines for those who would be kings. What three things are especially to be avoided?

These will serve as useful "performance indicators" for our new king. Keep them in mind; we'll come back to them in our next study.

 **GOING FURTHER**

1.  How does Solomon's glorious reign compare with Jesus? Look up Matthew 12:42; 27:37; 28:18. How was Jesus less glorious than Solomon? How was He more glorious?

2. Under the rule of David and Solomon, the borders of Israel grew to encompass the small surrounding nations. What is the scope of the rule of King Jesus?

3. What does it mean in practical terms that Jesus has this authority over you?

4. In the light of the great authority given Him through His death and resurrection (Matt. 28:18), what does Jesus call His disciples to do (v. 19)?

5. God has done a great job of keeping His promises: David and Solomon have both said so in their own words. And, in spite of a few stumbles, David and Solomon have been holding things together pretty well. Since they are the main representatives of Israel we've looked at in this study, give Israel a faithfulness rating based on the performance of its kings.

1    2    3    4    5    6    7    8    9    10

# 6

# The Kingdom Goes

## Solomon–Exile

 **STARTING OUT**

Think about your own experiences of life. Are you more likely to forget about God when things are going well or when things are going poorly? Why is that?

### Going Up, Coming Down

"What goes up must come down!" It's true of many things—airplanes, Frisbees, umbrellas, socks. Unfortunately, it was also true of King Solomon.

In our last study we examined King Solomon on his way up. Israel was having economic and military success and was growing in cultural sophistication. Everyone wanted to go to Israel for their holidays. Money was pouring into the country because businesses wanted to invest in Israel. All the rulers of the world were lining up to have their photo taken with King Solomon of Israel. Solomon was *Time* magazine's "Man of the Year." It looked as if all of God's promises to Israel had finally come true.

God promised Abraham that He would make his descendants into a great nation and bless them in their own land. Under Solomon it seemed as if it had all finally happened. In 2 Samuel 7, God promised King David that his family would rule over His people forever. Under Solomon it seemed as if that promise had been fulfilled. This was Israel's golden age.

But what goes up usually comes down. King Solomon goes up like a skyrocket and comes down like a lead weight.

 **FINDING TRUTH**

1. Think back to the three guidelines for kings that we discovered in Deuteronomy 17. (We looked at them in the last study.) Let's see how Solomon fares . . .

   STRIKE 1
   Read 1 Kings 10:26 and 28. What has Solomon forgotten?

   STRIKE 2
   Read 1 Kings 10:27. What has Solomon forgotten?

   STRIKE 3
   Read 1 Kings 11:1-8. What has Solomon forgotten?

2.  What does God promise to do as punishment (11:9-13)?

3.  Read 1 Kings 12:1-24. What are the political reasons for the splitting apart of Israel? What are the underlying spiritual reasons?

## The Bubble Bursts

Even in our last study we noted several aspects about David and Solomon that made us suspicious of how firm Israel's faithfulness was. In 1 Kings 10–11, however, it becomes clear that Israel and her rulers are far from being as faithful as they should be. In spite of the fact that God has spoken to him in person, and has spelled out His requirements in His law, Solomon has chosen the path of unfaithfulness. He starts to hoard gold; he gathers chariots and horses, putting his confidence in the might of his army rather than the might of God. And worst of all, Solomon marries foreign women who lead his heart away from God. Solomon is mirroring the very same sin that has been Israel's downfall all along. Despite God's command, they have consistently refused to follow Him wholeheartedly.

The consequences are disastrous! From here on, the books of 1 and 2 Kings trace the decline of the once-great kingdom of Israel.

Let's take it step by step. After Solomon's son Rehoboam takes the throne, there's a civil war. The northern tribes rebel, and the nation of Israel splits into two halves. The northern section retains the name Israel, elects a new king named Jeroboam (who is not from the family of David) and sets up a new capital at Samaria. Jeroboam also establishes altars at Dan and Bethel and urges the people to worship there rather than at the temple in Jerusalem.

The southern tribe of Judah retains David's family as their rulers, they remain with Jerusalem as their capital city, and they keep the temple. But things are never the same. The golden age of Israel is now over.

The rest of 1 and 2 Kings describes the separate fates of the northern and southern kingdoms. It can all get a bit confusing as we jump from one kingdom to the other, but for the moment let's just stick with the story of the northern kingdom.

 **FINDING TRUTH**

1. How do the kings of Israel seem to be going?

   ▲ 1 Kings 15:25-26


   ▲ 1 Kings 15:33-34


   ▲ 1 Kings 16:29-33


   ▲ 1 Kings 22:51-53


2. Much of 1—2 Kings is devoted to the ministry of the prophets Elijah and Elisha. Both of these men warned the people of Israel (the northern kingdom) about the consequences of rejecting God's law. What is Elijah's assessment of how things are going? See 1 Kings 19:10.

3. Amos and Hosea were another two prophets who tried to call Israel to repentance. How does Hosea think Israel is doing? See Hosea 4:1-3.

4. Read 2 Kings 17:1-23. What happens to Israel and why?

## Israel: The Northern Kingdom

The history of the northern kingdom is a sorry tale indeed. The pattern is set by their first king, Jeroboam. Not only did Jeroboam reject God's word by becoming king in the first place (he wasn't a descendant of David) but he also rejected God's temple in Jerusalem and led the people to worship idols. All the other kings followed in Jeroboam's footsteps, and Israel sank into a pit of immorality and apostasy. Under God's judgment, the northern kingdom of Israel was eventually crushed by the Assyrian Empire and disappeared from the pages of history.

Maybe things are going better in the southern kingdom . . .

 **FINDING TRUTH**

1. What are the kings of Judah like? Here's a sample:
   ▲ 2 Kings 8:16-19

   ▲ 2 Kings 16:1-4

   ▲ 2 Kings 18:1-4

   ▲ 2 Kings 21:1-6

(Still not sure? Then also have a look at 2 Kings 12:1-3; 15:1-4; 21:19-22; 22:1-2; 23:31-32.)

2. Jeremiah was one of the prophets who brought God's message to Judah. Look at Jeremiah 11:1-13. What is Jeremiah's message and what is it based on?

3. Read 2 Kings 25:1-26. What happens to Judah?

4. How are God's promises to Abraham going by the end of 1—2 Kings?

## Judah: The Southern Kingdom

Despite retaining kings from David's family and centering their worship at the temple in Jerusalem, the southern kingdom also degenerates into rebellion against God. Although some of the kings, such as Josiah, try to turn the people's hearts back to God, they are unsuccessful. Even warnings from prophets such as Isaiah, Jeremiah, and Ezekiel aren't enough. Judah continually falls victim to the same sin as Solomon—they turn their hearts to other gods and they are not fully devoted to the Lord their God.

Way back in Deuteronomy God had warned His people of what would happen if they deserted Him (Deut. 28:15-68). God said that He would punish them by driving them out of the Promised Land. They would be enslaved in a foreign land. And that's exactly what happened.

In the event known as "the Exile," Judah was conquered by the Babylonian Empire. Jerusalem was destroyed, the temple was leveled, and thousands of prisoners were taken back to Babylon as exiles. (Daniel is an example of one such exile.)

By the end of 2 Kings, Israel is in utter shambles. Idolatry and immorality has been punished with civil war and conquest. In the space of 27 chapters Israel has gone from the heights of their golden age under Solomon to the gloomy depths of the Exile.

Is this the end for Israel? What of God's promises? Stay tuned for the next study.

## The Kings Are Dead, Long Live the King!

If you visit a jeweler and ask to look at some diamonds, more often than not the jeweler will show you the diamonds against a black velvet cloth. The dark background is useful because it emphasizes the brightness and beauty of the diamond. That's what the books of 1 and 2 Kings do for Jesus Christ. The gloom and darkness of Israel's sinful kings serve to highlight the beauty of Christ's kingship.

Most of Israel's kings were selfish, evil leaders who led the people away from the true and living God. In the words of Ezekiel, they were like harsh and brutal shepherds who cared nothing for the sheep (Ezek. 34). Jesus, however, is the Good Shepherd who properly cares for His flock (John 10). Jesus leads with self-sacrificing love—a love that would even take Him to the Cross.

For those of us who live this side of the Cross, then, even this depressing period of Israel's history has an exciting dimension to it. As we see Israel's kings at their worst, it forces us to look forward to a more satisfying fulfillment of God's promises to Abraham.

**GOING FURTHER**

1.  If Solomon was so wise, how could he go so wrong? Are there any warnings here for us?

2.  Throughout this period of history, Israel and her kings refuse to be God's holy people. As followers of Jesus, we also are called to be holy (1 Pet. 1:13-16).

    a.  What does this mean in practical terms?

    b.  How are you doing in this regard? Is there any real difference between your life and attitudes and those of your non-Christian friends? Why or why not?

3.  Throughout this period of history, are there any kings who really stick in your mind? Why?

4.  Have you ever doubted that Jesus is a good leader? Why or why not?

# 7

# Is God Dead?

## The Exile

 **STARTING OUT**

The words *Exodus* and *Exile* appear to be quite similar. The events are very different! From what you already know of the Exile (see previous study) list as many differences as you can between the events of the Exodus and the Exile.

## An Absent God?

In the late 1960s, *Time* magazine ran a famous headline. It was a period of history when America was gripped by the fear of communism and the threat of nuclear war. Social unrest was spreading like a cancer as political and racial riots erupted throughout the country. Martin Luther King, Jr., had been shot to death in Memphis. President John F. Kennedy had been shot to death in Dallas. Senator Robert Kennedy had been shot to death in Los Angeles.

In the midst of all this national distress, *Time* was published with a black cover containing three simple words in white: "Is God Dead?" It seemed the obvious question to ask. If God was there, then why wasn't He doing something? Why was the world in such a mess? Didn't God care? Was He dead?

In this study we enter a time of Israel's history when questions like these were on the lips of every Israelite.

## FINDING TRUTH

1.  Lamentations is a book written at the time of the Exile. Read Lamentations 1. What reasons are given for the Exile?

2.  What emotional effect did the Exile have on the people of Judah? Why do you think it had such a big impact?

3.  Read Lamentations 3:19-33. Amid great despair, what is the writer's basis for hope?

## By the Waters of Babylon We Wept

As we discovered in study 6, Judah has been punished for her sinfulness by being conquered by the Babylonian Empire. Jerusalem and the temple have been destroyed, thousands of prisoners have been dragged off to Babylon to live as exiles, and the Israelites are in utter despair and confusion.

How could God do something like this? What about all His promises to Abraham—promises that the Israelites would be a blessed nation in their own land? Now they are exiles in a foreign land. It's a complete disaster. The only other Old Testament event to rival the tragedy of the Exile was the Fall, when Adam and Eve rebelled in the Garden of Eden. Indeed, there are strong similarities between the Fall and the Exile. In both cases God's special people rebel against His rule and are thrown out of their special land as punishment. History is repeating itself—sin has again reared its ugly head.

The big question is: Has God totally given up on Israel, or does He plan to restore it? The answer can be found in the words of the prophets who proclaimed God's Word in the time leading up to and even including the Exile. Among these prophets were Jeremiah, Ezekiel, and Isaiah.

 **FINDING TRUTH**

1. According to the prophets, what will happen after the Exile?

   ▲ Isaiah 65:17-25

   ▲ Jeremiah 16:14-15

   ▲ Jeremiah 29:10-14

   ▲ Jeremiah 31:31-34

   ▲ Ezekiel 36:33-36

   ▲ Ezekiel 37:21-28

2.  Within these future plans for God's people, two specific individuals will play an important role. Who are they and what do they do?

    ▲ Person 1: Isaiah 11:1-5; Jeremiah 33:14-26

    ▲ Person 2: Isaiah 52:13–53:12

## A Brave New World

Despite the gloom of the Exile, the prophets never gave up hope for a future fulfillment of God's promises to Abraham and King David. Indeed, the grandeur of what God was to do after the Exile would make everything that came before pale into insignificance. Israel was going to enjoy a rescue from Babylon that would surpass even the Exodus (Jer. 16:14-15). A new covenant would now be established in which sin would be forgiven and, best of all, God would give His people a new heart, through which they would actually desire to do good (Jer. 31).

These are majestic promises! Through His prophets God has recommitted Himself to breaking sin's stranglehold on humanity. The result will be a new heaven and a new earth in which the harmony and peace of the Garden of Eden will be recaptured (Isa. 65:17ff.).

Within this new creation, two specific individuals will play very significant roles. The first is a new Davidic king, who will rule his people in righteousness and justice. The second is a mysterious servant, whose suffering will somehow lead to the forgiveness of sins. We'll have more to say about these two people later, but for now let's investigate what practical implications these promises have for the exiles in captivity.

**FINDING TRUTH**

1. Read Jeremiah 29:1-9.

   a. How should the exiles respond to the Exile?

   b. Why do you think this advice is given (see vv. 10-11)?

2. Read Daniel 3. What lessons do you see here about how the exiles are to live in Babylon?

3. Read Daniel 9:1-19. According to Daniel, how should the exiles now respond to God?

4. What signs of comfort can be seen in the experiences of Daniel and his colleagues?

## Aliens in a Foreign Land

While the Israelites were in exile, the prophets encouraged them to repent and return to God. It was Israel's blatant sinfulness that had led God to cause the Exile; it was a painful but necessary disciplinary event. The appropriate response, then, was for the people to learn from the discipline and renew their devotion to God. Israel was therefore called on to settle into normal life in Babylon—but never in such a way as to compromise their commitment to God.

The words of the prophets and the example of people like Daniel and his friends encouraged the Israelites to repent and once again live the life of faith. They were to look beyond their present circumstances, trust in God's promises for the future, and therefore refuse to compromise on following God. This was exactly the same lifestyle the Israelites had been taught to live in the wilderness (study 3) but which they had failed in dismally during their occupancy of the Promised Land (study 6). The question remains as to whether the Exile experience will teach the Israelites to learn from their mistakes.

## The Servant King

In study 2 we already noted that Jesus Christ is the ultimate fulfillment of all of God's promises (2 Cor. 1:20). The prophetic promises we have investigated in this study are no exception.

Christ ushers in the new covenant through His death on the Cross (Luke 22:20). By His death He secures forgiveness of sins and enables a deep relationship with God in which His Spirit transforms and shapes our hearts (Rom. 8:1-4; Gal. 5:16-26).

As we've discovered in this study, the new Davidic king and the suffering servant of God—the king who will rule God's people with righteousness and the servant who will somehow provide for the forgiveness of sins—both seem to have a key role in establishing the new covenant. In God's infinite wisdom and foreknowledge, Jesus Christ fulfilled both of these roles. Jesus appeared as the Messiah, the divinely anointed ruler of God's people. Yet Jesus is a king who rules His people by serving them. He went to the Cross to suffer in our place. Our Servant King was indeed "pierced for our transgressions" and "crushed for our iniquities" (Isa. 53:5).

## GOING FURTHER

1.  The modern Christian's position is quite similar to that of the exiles in Babylon. We are aliens in a land that is not our ultimate home. How does the promise of our heavenly home help us deal with life? (See Rom. 8:18-39; 2 Thess. 1:5-10.)

2.  What pressures do we face to compromise our faith in Christ?

3.  What words of advice does 1 Peter 2:11-12 offer? What specific things can we do to put this advice into practice?

4.  Christ is both the anointed Messiah and the suffering servant of God. How do these two aspects of Christ's role spur us on to greater obedience?

5.  Recall a time when things have not gone well for you.
    ▲ What sorts of thoughts did you have?

    ▲ How did you feel toward God?

▲ Does Israel's experience of the Exile provide any lessons about God which might help us deal with such times?

6. Is God still being faithful to His promises? Update His rating.

7. Things haven't gone well for the people of Israel. They're paying the consequences for their past unfaithfulness. But maybe they've learned their lesson? Maybe you've seen some signs of progress? Maybe they've turned the corner? Update Israel's faithfulness rating to reflect your opinion on their current state.

8. How would you rate your own faithfulness to God?

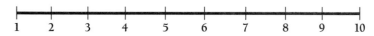

# A Diary of Disaster

## NEHEMIAH

 **STARTING OUT**

Look back to the timeline you created at the start of this book. How accurate was your picture of the Old Testament? What events were at the end of your timeline?

## Happy Endings

Movies don't always have happy endings. Have you ever seen *Butch Cassidy and the Sundance Kid?* You may remember it as the film that made stars of Robert Redford and Paul Newman; you may remember it as the film that made a hit of the song "Raindrops Keep Falling on My Head." But most probably, you'll remember it for its devastating ending. Our likeable cowboy heroes are actually villains, and they're finally surrounded by hundreds of soldiers and lawmen. Butch and Sundance storm out of their hiding place to face overwhelming odds. A volley of shots rings out . . . and the credits roll down the screen.

A memorable ending? Yes. A happy ending? No.

It's much the same with the Old Testament. Though there have been high points, though there have been hopeful signs, though God's faithfulness has been unquestionable, the human heroes have always had a fatal flaw. And in the end, it's a flaw that brings disaster.

The books of Ezra and Nehemiah record the final phases of Old Testament history. Along with prophets such as Zechariah and Malachi, these books describe Israel's resettlement in the Promised Land after the terrible Babylonian exile.

In this study we'll focus mainly on Nehemiah; in your spare time, you might like to read through Ezra for additional background.

 **FINDING TRUTH**

1.  Read through Nehemiah 1.

    What can you discover about the historical setting of the book?

2.  As we have worked through the Old Testament, we have been reminded of the significance of God's promises to Abraham. What does Nehemiah say about this "covenant"?

3.  Nehemiah quotes from Deuteronomy 30:4-10. What promises did God make in that passage for the specific situation Israel now faces?

4.  What questions does this raise about Israel's future in the land?

## Rebuilding the Wall

As we have discovered, Nehemiah is a high-ranking official in the court of the Persian king (1:11). On hearing the news that the rebuilding of Jerusalem is not going well, Nehemiah is driven to prayer.

In chapter 2, Nehemiah gains the king's blessing to return to Jerusalem and help supervise the rebuilding project. Under his leadership, the huge project of rebuilding the city walls—a task that dominates the book—is soon under way. Why does the city need walls? It needs them to keep out the surrounding enemies; but more than that, perhaps, the walls are symbolic of a boundary marking out the people of God from the peoples round about.

For Nehemiah, at least, the walls are a concrete reminder of God's covenant promises to Abraham—especially the promise that the land of Israel and the city of Jerusalem will be the secure home of God's faithful people. "If the people repent, I will bring them back to the land and bless them," said God (see Deut. 30:4-5). And Nehemiah is taking God's promise seriously.

After fifty-two days of hard work, the walls of Jerusalem are finally completed. By the end of chapter 7, God's people are secure in the Promised Land, each in his or her own town. God's promise to restore His people has been fulfilled. But the question remains: Will the newly resettled people of Israel be as faithful to God as God has been to them?

**FINDING TRUTH**

1.  In Nehemiah 9, the Levites lead a public assembly in prayer and recount the whole sorry tale of God's covenant blessing and Israel's repeated unfaithfulness. Read chapter 9. Work through the history detailed in the Levites' prayer (events that should be familiar by now!) and fill in the verse numbers in chapter 9 that mark out each section:

    ▲ Creation (vv. ____ to ____)

    ▲ The promises to Abraham (vv. ____ to ____)

    ▲ The Exodus from Egypt (vv. ____ to ____)

    ▲ The Law given on Sinai (vv. ____ to ____)

2.  What happened then? (vv. 16-17)

3.  How did God respond?

    ▲ Wandering in the desert (vv. ____ to ____)

    ▲ Taking the Promised Land (vv. ____ to ____)

4.  What happened then? (vv. 26-27)

5.  How did God respond when they repented? (v. 27)

6. Verse 28 summarizes the whole routine. How many times did this happen?

7. Why didn't God simply put an end to the stiff-necked Israelites? (v. 31)

8. The people of Israel are obviously cut to the heart by this account of the sins of their forefathers. As they call out to God to save them once more from their bondage (remember, they're still under foreign control) they decide to make a binding contract with God (v. 38). What do the Israelites now promise? (10:29) List the three key issues this will involve:

▲ 10:30

▲ 10:31

▲ 10:32-39

## Rebuilding Their Holiness

Things are looking promising. The new walls are dedicated in a glorious celebration that recalls the golden age of King David. (Notice how often his name is mentioned in 12:27-47.) The temple store rooms are full to overflowing. What's more, the Israelites have promised that they will again become the holy and unique people God intended them to be, obeying all His laws and statutes.

It certainly seems that things are finally sorting themselves out. The high expectations of the prophets (see study 7) seem to be well founded. By this time—after twelve years of hard work—Nehemiah figures it is safe to take a trip back to Babylon to report to the king. He spends some time there, then makes the long trip back to Jerusalem. You'll never guess what he discovers when he returns!

## FINDING TRUTH

1.   What has happened in Nehemiah's absence?

▲   13:10-11

▲   13:15-16

▲   13:23-24

2.   How does Nehemiah react? (See vv. 11, 17-22, 25-28.)

## A Dismal End to the Diary

After building the wall and struggling to reestablish a faithful Israel, all of Nehemiah's efforts are laid to ruin by the absolute inability of the people of Israel to keep their covenant with God. Yes, the city walls have been rebuilt—but the city's *people* have not. Nehemiah gave it his best shot, but in the end his diary is a diary of disaster. And so, the account of the history of Israel ends on a dismal note indeed, with Israel having stepped right into the same sins as Solomon (13:26-27). Nehemiah is left begging God for a pardon (13:14, 22, 31).

To borrow the words of T. S. Eliot, the Old Testament ends "not with a bang but a whimper."

## The Old Testament and Jesus Christ

In a very real sense, therefore, the Exile does not end in the Old Testament (see Luke 2:25). Despite Nehemiah's best efforts, the promises of a new exodus, a new creation, and a new covenant (study 7) are not achieved. The disappointment is great. But for us, living this side of the Cross, the excitement is also great because we are now in a position to appreciate the way in which the entire Old Testament points us toward and prepares us for Jesus Christ. For it is precisely in the disappointment of the Old Testament that we discover our need for Christ.

The great tragedy of the Old Testament is that, although there is nothing God wants more than to gather a people to Himself, humanity keeps pushing Him away. The rebellion started with Adam and Eve at the Fall, and it has persisted all through the Old Testament as the Israelites and their kings simply don't want to be the unique nation God has called them to be. Rather than maintain their national distinctiveness—their holiness—they play "mix-and-match" with the surrounding nations.

The Old Testament therefore points us to the need for God to do something definitive about sin. If God is ever going to reverse the Fall and keep His promises to Abraham, sin has to be dealt with once and for all. It is with this thought in mind that the curtains of the New Testament open and Jesus Christ steps into history. The Son of God Himself comes to deal decisively with sin. By dying in our place on the Cross, Jesus takes the punishment we deserve. We are given a fresh start.

What's more, we're given a fresh *heart*. Through God's Spirit our lives are changed so that we actually want to do His will in a way that the Israelites living before the Cross could never experience. That's not to say that our obedience to God is automatic; until we reach perfection in heaven, it will be a struggle. And yet we have the resources we need to meet the challenge.

In Christ, therefore, all the promises of God are fulfilled. As God promised Abraham, a blessed people of God are gathered together (1 Pet. 2:9-10). As God promised David, one of David's descendants will rule forever in justice and righteousness (Acts 2:29-36). As God promised through the prophets, a new covenant has been established (Luke 22:20).

How much Nehemiah would have enjoyed knowing the blessings that we enjoy through Christ!

 **GOING FURTHER**

1. Why was it so important that the Israelites not intermarry with other nations? What application can you see for this principle today? What often happens when this advice is ignored (see 2 Cor. 6:14)?

2. Read Hebrews 8:6-13 and 9:15.

   a. What is the problem with the old covenant? (8:8)

   b. What did God promise to do? (8:8b)

   c. In what way is the new covenant different? (8:10)

   d. There's one other key part of the "package deal." What is it? (8:12)

    e.    How does Christ's death make possible the promise of 8:12? (9:15)

    f.    How do *you* take part in this new covenant?

3.   As a follower of Jesus, do you see evidence of the fact that God's law is "written in your heart" (8:10)? How?

4.   If God's people in Old Testament times were called to be unique, even though their laws were only written on stone, what about us?

5. Congratulations! You made it through the Old Testament! We've followed the saga of Israel from start to finish. Have there been any sections that have particularly challenged or comforted you? Why?

6. From what you have discovered about God throughout these studies, give God a rating for His faithfulness to you:

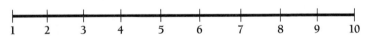

1   2   3   4   5   6   7   8   9   10

7. Now, give yourself a rating for your present faithfulness to God. What specific things can you be doing to improve on this rating?

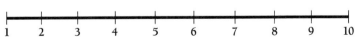

1   2   3   4   5   6   7   8   9   10

# *Tips for Leaders*

Most people, if they read the Old Testament at all, treat it like a phone book or a dictionary—a prooftext here, a half-remembered verse there, and the occasional riveting yarn about Noah or Samson or King David thrown in for good measure. But how does it all fit together?

The first step to appreciating the Old Testament is to understand that it contains a single unified story. It is the unfolding story of God's commitment to His promise to bless the world through the descendants of Abraham. The Old Testament is full of promise—and the promise is ultimately fulfilled in Jesus Christ.

Like any other piece of unified literature, the whole Old Testament therefore needs to be read in such a way that recurring themes and patterns are noticed and appreciated. That's what we hope to achieve through these studies. Large slabs of the Old Testament are dealt with so as to draw out the key themes and ideas. Indeed this is a good way to read any part of the Bible. For example, to truly appreciate each of the Gospels or any of the apostle Paul's letters, they are best read in one sitting. Approaching the Bible in this way helps us to see the "big picture."

Dipping into the Old Testament without understanding the big picture can lead to all sorts of problems. We end up with a fragmented understanding of the Old Testament and we never come to grips with the idea that, from the beginning of Genesis to the end of Nehemiah—the last stage in the account of Israel's history—it's a story that is going somewhere. As Christians, we especially need to be always ready to jump into the story line and follow it through to the logical destination—fulfillment in the life, death, resurrection, ascension, and kingly rule of Jesus Christ.

Because these studies are designed to highlight the overarching story line, the framework of the Old Testament, that means certain issues and events are not even mentioned. Try to avoid the temptation to add bits that you feel should have been included. We've worked hard to slim things down to a manageable outline. And if your group can catch hold of the framework now, you'll find that detailed study of parts of the Old Testament later on will be much easier. Knowing where things fit in the big picture is a big help in making sense of the Bible. So for now, be content with our "aerial view" and don't be tempted to get any closer!

Even with our best efforts to make the studies manageable, they're still a little more detailed than we would have liked. These studies will work best if your group prepares during the week. Not preparing ahead will mean that the group is unlikely to complete a study in a single session.

Getting a hold on the sweep of the Old Testament story is exciting. You'll marvel at the way the plot line fits together. You'll groan at the constant failings of Israel. And most of all, you'll be thrilled at the way all the promises of God find their fulfillment in Christ.

Ask your local bookstore about these other
FaithWalk Bible Studies

**Beginnings**
Eden and Beyond: Genesis 1–11

**Deuteronomy**
The Lord Your God

**Isaiah**
The Road to God

**Daniel**
Our Faithful God

**The Beatitudes**
A Guide to Good Living: Matthew 5:1-12

**Mark**
The Beginning of the Gospel

**Galatians**
The Gospel of Grace

**Ephesians**
Our Blessings in Christ

**Colossians**
Continuing in Christ

**1 Timothy**
The Household of God

**James**
Life in the Real World

# Notes

# Notes

## About Matthias Media

This Bible study guide, part of the *FaithWalk Bible Studies,* was originally developed and published in Australia by Matthias Media. Matthias Media is an evangelical publisher focusing on producing resources for Christian ministry. For further information about Matthias Media products, visit their website at: www.matthiasmedia.com.au; or contact them by E-mail at: matmedia@ozemail.com.au; or by fax at: 61-2-9662-4289.